THIS COLORING BOOK BELONG TO:

....

....

MILK

www.vecteezy.com

www.vecteezy.com

www.vecteezy.com

www.vecteezy.com

www.vecteezy.com

www.vecteezy.com

www.vecteezy.com

www.vecteezy.com

www.vecteezy.com

www.vecteezy.com

www.vecteezy.com

www.vecteezy.com

www.vecteezy.com

www.vecteezy.com

www.vecteezy.com

best friends

www.vecteezy.com

Meow